THE GOLDEN THRESHOLD

By

SAROJINI NAIDU

WITH A CHAPTER FROM
Studies of Contemporary Poets
BY MARY C. STURGEON

First published in 1905

Copyright © 2020 Ragged Hand

This edition is published by Ragged Hand,
an imprint of Read & Co.

This book is copyright and may not be reproduced or copied in any way without the express permission of the publisher in writing.

British Library Cataloguing-in-Publication Data
A catalogue record for this book is available
from the British Library.

Read & Co. is part of Read Books Ltd.
For more information visit
www.readandcobooks.co.uk

DEDICATED TO EDMUND GOSSE,
WHO FIRST SHOWED ME THE WAY
TO THE GOLDEN THRESHOLD.

London, 1896
Hyderabad, 1905

CONTENTS

SAROJINI NAIDU
By Mary C. Sturgeon................................7

INTRODUCTION.................................17

FOLK SONGS

PALANQUIN BEARERS............................25

WANDERING SINGERS............................26

INDIAN WEAVERS................................27

COROMANDEL FISHERS...........................28

THE SNAKE-CHARMER............................29

CORN-GRINDERS.................................30

VILLAGE-SONG..................................32

IN PRAISE OF HENNA............................33

HARVEST HYMN.................................34

INDIAN LOVE-SONG.............................36

CRADLE-SONG..................................37

SUTTEE...38

SONGS FOR MUSIC

SONG OF A DREAM..............................39

HUMAYUN TO ZOBEIDA..........................40

AUTUMN SONG..................................41

ALABASTER.....................................42

ECSTASY..43

TO MY FAIRY FANCIES...........................44

POEMS

ODE TO H.H. THE NIZAM OF HYDERABAD 45

LEILI 47

IN THE FOREST 48

PAST AND FUTURE 49

LIFE 50

THE POET'S LOVE-SONG 51

TO THE GOD OF PAIN 52

THE SONG OF PRINCESS ZEB-UN-NISSA
IN PRAISE OF HER OWN BEAUTY 53

INDIAN DANCERS 54

MY DEAD DREAM 55

DAMAYANTE TO NALA IN THE HOUR OF EXILE ... 56

THE QUEEN'S RIVAL 58

THE POET TO DEATH 61

THE INDIAN GIPSY 62

TO MY CHILDREN 63

THE PARDAH NASHIN 65

TO YOUTH 66

NIGHTFALL IN THE CITY OF HYDERABAD 67

STREET CRIES 68

TO INDIA 69

THE ROYAL TOMBS OF GOLCONDA 70

TO A BUDDHA SEATED ON A LOTUS 71

Sarojini Naidu

By Mary C. Sturgeon

Mrs Naidu is one of the two Indian poets who within the last few years have produced remarkable English poetry. The second of the two is, of course, Rabindranath Tagore, whose work has come to us a little later, who has published more, and whose recent visit to this country has brought him more closely under the public eye. Mrs Naidu is not so well known; but she deserves to be, for although the bulk of her work is not so large, its quality, so far as it can be compared with that of her compatriot, will easily bear the test. It is, however, so different in kind, and reveals a genius so contrasting, that one is piqued by an apparent problem. How is it that two children of what we are pleased to call the changeless East, under conditions nearly identical, should have produced results which are so different?

Both of these poets are lyrists born; both come of an old and distinguished Bengali ancestry; in both the culture of East and West are happily met; and both are working in the same artistic medium. Yet the poetry of Rabindranath Tagore is mystical, philosophic, and contemplative, remaining oriental therefore to that degree; and permitting a doubt of the *Quarterly* reviewer's dictum that "Gitanjali"is a synthesis of western and oriental elements. The complete synthesis would seem to rest with Mrs Naidu, whose poetry, though truly native to her motherland, is more sensuous than mystical, human and passionate rather than spiritual, and reveals a mentality more active than contemplative. Her affiliation with the Occident is so much the more complete; but her Eastern origin is never in doubt.

The themes of her verse and their setting are derived from

her own country. But her thought, with something of the energy of the strenuous West and something of its 'divine discontent,' plays upon the surface of an older and deeper calm which is her birthright. So, in her "Salutation to the Eternal Peace," she sings

> What care I for the world's loud weariness,
> Who dream in twilight granaries
> Thou dost bless
> With delicate sheaves of mellow silences?

Two distinguished poet-friends of Mrs Naidu—Mr Edmund Gosse and Mr Arthur Symons—have introduced her two principal volumes of verse with interesting biographical notes. The facts thus put in our possession convey a picture to the mind which is instantly recognizable in the poems.

A gracious and glowing personality appears, quick and warm with human feeling, exquisitely sensitive to beauty and receptive of ideas, wearing its culture, old and new, scientific and humane, with simplicity; but, as Mr Symons says, "a spirit of too much fire in too frail a body," and one moreover who has suffered and fought to the limit of human endurance.

We hear of birth and childhood in Hyderabad; of early scientific training by a father whose great learning was matched by his public spirit: of a first poem at the age of eleven, written in an impulse of reaction when a sum in algebra *would not come right*: of coming to England at the age of sixteen with a scholarship from the Nizam college; and of three years spent here, studying at King's College, London, and at Girton, with glorious intervals of holiday in Italy.

We hear, too, of a love-story that would make an idyll; of passion so strong and a will so resolute as almost to be incredible in such a delicate creature; of a marriage in defiance of caste, a few years of brilliant happiness and then a tragedy. And all through, as a dark background to the adventurous romance of her life, there is the shadow of weakness and ill-health. That shadow creeps into her poems, impressively, now and then. Indeed, if it were lacking, the bright oriental colouring would be almost too vivid. So, apart from its psychological and human interest, we may be thankful for such a poem as "To the God of Pain." It softens and deepens the final impression of the work.

> For thy dark altars, balm nor milk nor rice,
> But mine own soul thou'st ta'en for sacrifice.

The poem is purely subjective, of course, as is the still more moving piece, "The Poet to Death," in the same volume.

> Tarry a while, till I am satisfied
> Of love and grief, of earth and altering sky;
> Till all my human hungers are fulfilled,
> O Death, I cannot die!

We know that that is a cry out of actual and repeated experience; and from that point of view alone it has poignant interest. But what are we to say about the spirit of it—the philosophy which is implicit in it? Here is an added value of a higher kind, evidence of a mind which has taken its own stand upon reality, and which has no easy consolations when confronting the facts of existence. For this mind, neither the religions of East nor West are allowed to veil the truth; neither the hope of Nirvana nor the promise of Paradise may drug her sense of the value of life nor darken her perception of the beauty of phenomena. Resignation and renunciation are alike impossible to this ardent being who loves the earth so passionately; but the 'sternly scientific' nature of that early training—the description is her own—has made futile regret impossible, too. She has entered into full possession of the thought of our time; and strongly individual as she is, she has evolved for herself, to use her own words, a "subtle philosophy of living from moment to moment." That is no shallow epicureanism, however, for as she sings in a poem contrasting our changeful life with the immutable peace of the Buddha on his lotus-throne—

> Nought shall conquer or control
> The heavenward hunger of our soul.

It is as though, realizing that the present is the only moment of which we are certain, she had determined to crowd that moment to the utmost limit of living.

From such a philosophy, materialism of a nobler kind, one would expect a love of the concrete and tangible, a delight in sense impressions, and quick and strong emotion. Those are, in fact, the characteristics of much of the poetry in these two volumes, *The Golden Threshold* and *The Bird of Time*. The beauty of the material world, of line and especially of colour, is caught and recorded joyously. Life is regarded mainly from the outside, in action, or as a pageant; as an interesting event or a picturesque group. It is not often brooded over, and reflection is generally evident in but the lightest touches. The proportion of strictly subjective verse is small, and is not, on the whole, the finest work technically.

The introspective note seems unfavourable to Mrs Naidu's art: naturally so, one would conclude, from the buoyant temperament that is revealed. The love-songs are perhaps an exception, for one or two, which (as we know) treat fragments of the poet's own story, are fine in idea and in technique alike. There is, for example, "An Indian Love Song," in the first stanza of which the lover begs for his lady's love. But she reminds him of the barriers of caste between them; she is afraid to profane the laws of her father's creed; and her lover's kinsmen, in times past, have broken the altars of her people and slaughtered their sacred kine. The lover replies:

> What are the sins of my race, Beloved, what are my
>   people to thee?
> And what are thy shrine, and kine and kindred, what are
>   thy gods to me?
> Love recks not of feuds and bitter follies, of stranger,
>   comrade orkin,
> Alike in his ear sound the temple bells and the cry of
>   the muezzin.

There is also in the second volume the "Dirge," in which the poet mourns the death of the husband whom she had dared to marry against the laws of caste; and which almost unconsciously reveals the influence of centuries of Suttee upon the mind of Indian womanhood.

> Shatter her shining bracelets, break the string
> Threading the mystic marriage-beads that cling
> Loth to desert a sobbing throat so sweet,
> Unbind the golden anklets on her feet,
> Divest her of her azure veils and cloud
> Her living beauty in a living shroud.

Even here, however, the effect is gained by colour and movement; by the grouping of images rather than by the development of an idea; and that will be found to be Mrs Naidu's method in the many delightful lyrics of these volumes where she is most successful. The "Folk Songs" of her first book are an example. One assumes that they are early work, partly because they are the first group in the earlier of the two volumes; but more particularly because they adopt so literally the advice which Mr Edmund Gosse gave her at the beginning of her career. When she came as a girl to England and was a student of London University at King's College, she submitted to Mr Gosse a bundle of manuscript poems. He describes them as accurate and careful work, but too derivative; modelled too palpably on the great poets of the previous generation. His advice, therefore, was that they should be destroyed, and that the author should start afresh upon native themes and in her own manner. The counsel was exactly followed: the manuscript went into the wastepaper basket, and the poet set to work on what we cannot doubt is this first group of songs made out of the lives of her own people.

There is all the hemisphere between these lyrics and those of late-Victorian England. Here we find a "Village Song" of a mother to the little bride who is still all but a baby; and to whom the fairies call so insistently that she will not stay "for bridal songs and bridal cakes and sandal-scented leisure." In the song of the "Palanquin Bearers" we positively see the lithe and rhythmic movements which bear some Indian beauty along, lightly "as a pearl on a string." And there is a song written to one of the tunes of those native minstrels who wander, free and wild as the wind, singing of

> The sword of old battles, the crown of old kings,
> And happy and simple and sorrowful things.

The "Harvest Hymn" raises thanksgiving for strange bounties to gods of unfamiliar names; and the "Cradle Song" evokes a tropical night, heavy with scent and drenched with dew—

> Sweet, shut your eyes,
> The wild fire-flies
> Dance through the fairy *neem*;
> From the poppy-bole,For you I stole
> A little, lovely dream.

In its lightness and grace, this poem is one of the exquisite things in our language: one of the little lyric flights, like William Watson's "April," which in their clear sweetness and apparent spontaneity are like some small bird's song. Mrs Naidu has said of herself—"I sing just as the birds do"; and as regards her loveliest lyrics (there are a fair proportion of them) she speaks a larger truth than she meant. Their simplicity and abandonment to the sheer joy of singing are infinitely refreshing; and fragile though they seem, one suspects them of great vitality. In the later volume there is another called "Golden Cassia"—the bright blooms that her people call mere 'woodland flowers.' The poet has other fancies about them; sometimes they seem to her like fragments of a fallen star—

> Or golden lamps for a fairy shrine,
> Or golden pitchers for fairy wine.
>
> Perchance you are, O frail and sweet!
> Bright anklet-bells from the wild spring's feet,
>
> Or the gleaming tears that some fair bride shed
> Remembering her lost maidenhead.

The tenderness and delicacy of verse like that might mislead us. We might suppose that the qualities of Mrs Naidu's work were only those which are arbitrarily known as feminine. But this poet, like Mrs Browning, is faithful to her own sensuous and passionate temperament. She has not timidly sheltered behind a convention which, because some women-poets have been austere, prescribes austerity, neutral tones, and a pale light for the woman-artist in this sphere. And, as a result, we have all the evidence of a richly-dowered sensibility responding frankly to the vivid light and colour, the liberal contours and rich scents and great spaces of the world she loves; and responding no less warmly and freely to human instincts. Occasionally her verse achieves the expression of sheer sensuous ecstasy. It does that, perhaps, in the two Dance poems—from the very reason that her art is so true and free. The theme requires exactly that treatment; and in "Indian Dancers" there is besides a curiously successful union between the measure that is employed and the subject of the poem—

> Their glittering garments of purple are burning like
> tremulous dawns inthe quivering air,
> And exquisite, subtle and slow are the tinkle and tread
> of their rhythmical, slumber-soft feet.

The love-songs, though in many moods, are always the frank expression of emotion that is deep and strong. One that is especially beautiful is the utterance of a young girl who, while her sisters prepare the rites for a religious festival, stands aside with folded hands dreaming of her lover. She is secretly asking herself what need has she to supplicate the gods, being blessed by love; and again, in the couple of stanzas called "Ecstasy," the rapture has passed, by its very intensity, into pain.

> Shelter my soul, O my love!
> My soul is bent low with the pain
> And the burden of love, like the grace
> Of a flower that is smitten with rain:
> O shelter my soul from thy face!

But, when all is said, it is the life of her people which inspires this poet most perfectly. In the lighter lyrics one sees the fineness of her touch; and in the love-poems the depth of her passion. But, in the folk-songs, all the qualities of her genius have contributed. Grace and tenderness have been reinforced by an observant eye, broad sympathy and a capacity for thought which reveals itself not so much as a systematic process as an atmosphere, suffusing the poems with gentle pensiveness. And always the artistic method is that of picking out the theme in bright sharp lines, and presenting the idea concretely, through the grouping of picturesque facts. There is a poem called "Street Cries" which is a vivid bit of the life of an Eastern city. First we have early morning, when the workers hurry out, fasting, to their toil; and the cry 'Buy bread, Buy bread' rings down the eager street; then midday, hot and thirsty, when the cry is 'Buy fruit, Buy fruit'; and finally, evening.

> When twinkling twilight o'er the gay bazaars,
> Unfurls a sudden canopy of stars,
> When lutes are strung and fragrant torches lit
> On white roof-terraces where lovers sit
> Drinking together of life's poignant sweet,
> *Buy flowers, buy flowers*, floats down the singing street.

Another of these shining pictures will be found in "Nightfall in the City of Hyderabad," Mrs Naidu's own city; and again in the song called "In a Latticed Balcony." But there are several others in which, added to the suggestion of an old civilization and strange customs, there is a haunting sense of things older and stranger still. Of such is this one, called "Indian Weavers."

> Weavers, weaving at break of day,
> Why do you weave a garment so gay? . . .
> Blue as the wing of a halcyon wild,
> We weave the robes of a new-born child.
>
> Weavers, weaving solemn and still,
> Why do you weave in the moonlight chill? . . .
> White as a feather and white as a cloud,
> We weave a dead man's funeral shroud.

A Chapter from
Studies of Contemporary Poets, 1916

INTRODUCTION

It is at my persuasion that these poems are now published. The earliest of them were read to me in London in 1896, when the writer was seventeen; the later ones were sent to me from India in 1904, when she was twenty-five; and they belong, I think, almost wholly to those two periods. As they seemed to me to have an individual beauty of their own, I thought they ought to be published. The writer hesitated. "Your letter made me very proud and very sad," she wrote. "Is it possible that I have written verses that are 'filled with beauty,' and is it possible that you really think them worthy of being given to the world? You know how high my ideal of Art is; and to me my poor casual little poems seem to be less than beautiful—I mean with that final enduring beauty that I desire." And, in another letter, she writes: "I am not a poet really. I have the vision and the desire, but not the voice. If I could write just one poem full of beauty and the spirit of greatness, I should be exultantly silent for ever; but I sing just as the birds do, and my songs are as ephemeral." It is for this bird-like quality of song, it seems to me, that they are to be valued. They hint, in a sort of delicately evasive way, at a rare temperament, the temperament of a woman of the East, finding expression through a Western language and under partly Western influences. They do not express the whole of that temperament; but they express, I think, its essence; and there is an Eastern magic in them.

Sarojini Chattopadhyay was born at Hyderabad on February 13, 1879. Her father, Dr. Aghorenath Chattopadhyay, is descended from the ancient family of Chattorajes of Bhramangram, who were noted throughout Eastern Bengal as patrons of Sanskrit learning, and for their practice of Yoga. He took his degree of

Doctor of Science at the University of Edinburgh in 1877, and afterwards studied brilliantly at Bonn. On his return to India he founded the Nizam College at Hyderabad, and has since laboured incessantly, and at great personal sacrifice, in the cause of education.

Sarojini was the eldest of a large family, all of whom were taught English at an early age. "I," she writes, "was stubborn and refused to speak it. So one day when I was nine years old my father punished me—the only time I was ever punished—by shutting me in a room alone for a whole day. I came out of it a full-blown linguist. I have never spoken any other language to him, or to my mother, who always speaks to me in Hindustani. I don't think I had any special hankering to write poetry as a little child, though I was of a very fanciful and dreamy nature. My training under my father's eye was of a sternly scientific character. He was determined that I should be a great mathematician or a scientist, but the poetic instinct, which I inherited from him and also from my mother (who wrote some lovely Bengali lyrics in her youth) proved stronger. One day, when I was eleven, I was sighing over a sum in algebra: it *wouldn't* come right; but instead a whole poem came to me suddenly. I wrote it down.

"From that day my 'poetic career' began. At thirteen I wrote a long poem a la 'Lady of the Lake'—1300 lines in six days. At thirteen I wrote a drama of 2000 lines, a full-fledged passionate thing that I began on the spur of the moment without forethought, just to spite my doctor who said I was very ill and must not touch a book. My health broke down permanently about this time, and my regular studies being stopped I read voraciously. I suppose the greater part of my reading was done between fourteen and sixteen. I wrote a novel, I wrote fat volumes of journals; I took myself very seriously in those days."

Before she was fifteen the great struggle of her life began. Dr. Govindurajulu Naidu, now her husband, is, though of an old and honourable family, not a Brahmin. The difference of caste roused an equal opposition, not only on the side of her family, but of his; and in 1895 she was sent to England, against her will, with a special scholarship from the Nizam. She remained in England, with an interval of travel in Italy, till 1898, studying first at King's College, London, then, till her health again broke down, at Girton. She returned to Hyderabad in September 1898, and in the December of that year, to the scandal of all India, broke through the bonds of caste, and married Dr. Naidu. "Do you know I have some very beautiful poems floating in the air," she wrote to me in 1904; "and if the gods are kind I shall cast my soul like a net and capture them, this year. If the gods are kind—and grant me a little measure of health. It is all I need to make my life perfect, for the very 'Spirit of Delight' that Shelley wrote of dwells in my little home; it is full of the music of birds in the garden and children in the long arched verandah." There are songs about the children in this book; they are called the Lord of Battles, the Sun of Victory, the Lotus-born, and the Jewel of Delight.

"My ancestors for thousands of years," I find written in one of her letters, "have been lovers of the forest and mountain caves, great dreamers, great scholars, great ascetics. My father is a dreamer himself, a great dreamer, a great man whose life has been a magnificent failure. I suppose in the whole of India there are few men whose learning is greater than his, and I don't think there are many men more beloved. He has a great white beard and the profile of Homer, and a laugh that brings the roof down. He has wasted all his money on two great objects: to help others, and on alchemy. He holds huge courts every day in his garden of all the learned men of all religions—Rajahs and beggars and saints and downright villains all delightfully mixed up, and all treated as one. And then his alchemy! Oh dear, night and day the experiments are going on, and every man who brings a new prescription is welcome as a brother. But this alchemy is, you know, only the material counterpart of a poet's craving for Beauty, the eternal Beauty. 'The makers of gold and the makers of verse,' they are the twin creators that sway the world's secret desire for mystery; and what in my father is the genius of curiosity—the very essence of all scientific genius—in me is the desire for beauty. Do you remember Pater's phrase about Leonardo da Vinci, 'curiosity and the desire of beauty'?"

It was the desire of beauty that made her a poet; her "nerves of delight" were always quivering at the contact of beauty. To those who knew her in England, all the life of the tiny figure seemed to concentrate itself in the eyes; they turned towards beauty as the sunflower turns towards the sun, opening wider and wider until one saw nothing but the eyes.

She was dressed always in clinging dresses of Eastern silk, and as she was so small, and her long black hair hung straight down her back, you might have taken her for a child. She spoke little, and in a low voice, like gentle music; and she seemed, wherever she was, to be alone.

Through that soul I seemed to touch and take hold upon the East. And first there was the wisdom of the East. I have never known any one who seemed to exist on such "large draughts of intellectual day" as this child of seventeen, to whom one could tell all one's personal troubles and agitations, as to a wise old woman. In the East, maturity comes early; and this child had already lived through all a woman's life. But there was something else, something hardly personal, something which belonged to a consciousness older than the Christian, which I realised, wondered at, and admired, in her passionate tranquillity of mind, before which everything mean and trivial and temporary caught fire and burnt away in smoke. Her body was never without suffering, or her heart without conflict; but neither the body's weakness nor the heart's violence could disturb that fixed contemplation, as of Buddha on his lotus-throne.

And along with this wisdom, as of age or of the age of a race, there was what I can hardly call less than an agony of sensation. Pain or pleasure transported her, and the whole of pain or pleasure might be held in a flower's cup or the imagined frown of a friend. It was never found in those things which to others seemed things of importance. At the age of twelve she passed the Matriculation of the Madras University, and awoke to find herself famous throughout India. "Honestly," she said to me, "I was not pleased; such things did not appeal to me." But here, in a letter from Hyderabad, bidding one "share a March morning" with her, there is, at the mere contact of the sun, this outburst: "Come and share my exquisite March morning with me: this sumptuous blaze of gold and sapphire sky; these scarlet lilies that adorn the sunshine; the voluptuous scents of neem and champak and serisha that beat upon the languid air with their implacable sweetness; the thousand little gold and blue and silver breasted birds bursting with the shrill ecstasy of life in nesting time. All is hot and fierce and passionate, ardent and unashamed in its exulting and importunate desire for life and love. And, do you know that the scarlet lilies are woven petal by petal from my heart's blood, these little quivering birds are my soul made incarnate music, these heavy perfumes are my emotions dissolved into aerial essence, this flaming blue and gold sky is the 'very me,' that part of me that incessantly and insolently, yes, and a little deliberately, triumphs over that other part—a thing of nerves and tissues that suffers and cries out, and that must die to-morrow perhaps, or twenty years hence."

Then there was her humour, which was part of her strange wisdom, and was always awake and on the watch. In all her letters, written in exquisite English prose, but with an ardent imagery and a vehement sincerity of emotion which make them, like the poems, indeed almost more directly, un-English, Oriental, there was always this intellectual, critical sense of humour, which could laugh at one's own enthusiasm as frankly as that enthusiasm had been set down. And partly the humour, like the delicate reserve of her manner, was a mask or a shelter. "I have taught myself," she writes to me from India, "to be commonplace and like everybody else superficially. Every one thinks I am so nice and cheerful, so 'brave,' all the banal things that are so comfortable to be. My mother knows me only as 'such a tranquil child, but so strong-willed.' A tranquil child!" And she writes again, with deeper significance: "I too have learnt the subtle philosophy of living from moment to moment. Yes, it is a subtle philosophy, though it appears merely an epicurean doctrine: 'Eat, drink, and be merry, for to-morrow we die.' I have gone through so many yesterdays when I strove with Death that I have realised to its full the wisdom of that sentence; and it is to me not merely a figure of speech, but a literal fact. Any to-morrow I might die. It is scarcely two months since I came back from the grave: is it worth while to be anything but radiantly glad? Of all things that life or perhaps my temperament has given me I prize the gift of laughter as beyond price."

Her desire, always, was to be "a wild free thing of the air like the birds, with a song in my heart." A spirit of too much fire in too frail a body, it was rarely that her desire was fully granted. But in Italy she found what she could not find in England, and from Italy her letters are radiant. "This Italy is made of gold," she writes from Florence, "the gold of dawn and daylight, the gold of the stars, and, now dancing in weird enchanting rhythms through this magic month of May, the gold of fireflies in the perfumed darkness—'aerial gold.' I long to catch the subtle music of their fairy dances and make a poem with a rhythm like the quick irregular wild flash of their sudden movements. Would it not be wonderful? One black night I stood in a garden with fireflies in my hair like darting restless stars caught in a mesh of darkness. It gave me a strange sensation, as if I were not human at all, but an elfin spirit. I wonder why these little things move me so deeply? It is because I have a most 'unbalanced intellect,' I suppose." Then, looking out on Florence, she cries, "God! how beautiful it is, and how glad I am that I am alive to-day!" And she tells me that she is drinking in the beauty like wine, "wine, golden and scented, and shining, fit for the gods; and the gods have drunk it, the dead gods of Etruria, two thousand years ago. Did I say dead? No, for the gods are immortal, and one might still find them loitering in some solitary dell on the grey hillsides of Fiesole. Have I seen them? Yes, looking with dreaming eyes, I have found them sitting under the olives, in their grave, strong, antique beauty—Etruscan gods!"

In Italy she watches the faces of the monks, and at one moment longs to attain to their peace by renunciation, longs for Nirvana; "then, when one comes out again into the hot sunshine that warms one's blood, and sees the eager hurrying faces of men and women in the street, dramatic faces over which the disturbing experiences of life have passed and left their symbols, one's heart thrills up into one's throat. No, no, no, a thousand times no! how can one deliberately renounce this coloured, unquiet, fiery human life of the earth?" And, all the time, her subtle criticism is alert, and this woman of the East marvels at the women of the West, "the beautiful worldly women of the West," whom she sees walking in the Cascine, "taking the air so consciously attractive in their brilliant toilettes, in the brilliant coquetry of their manner!" She finds them "a little incomprehensible," "profound artists in all the subtle intricacies of fascination," and asks if these "incalculable frivolities and vanities and coquetries and caprices" are, to us, an essential part of their charm? And she watches them with amusement as they flutter about her, petting her as if she were a nice child, a child or a toy, not dreaming that she is saying to herself sorrowfully: "How utterly empty their lives must be of all spiritual beauty IF they are nothing more than they appear to be."

She sat in our midst, and judged us, and few knew what was passing behind that face "like an awakening soul," to use one of her own epithets. Her eyes were like deep pools, and you seemed to fall through them into depths below depths.

ARTHUR SYMONS.

FOLK SONGS

PALANQUIN BEARERS

Lightly, O lightly we bear her along,
She sways like a flower in the wind of our song;
She skims like a bird on the foam of a stream,
She floats like a laugh from the lips of a dream.
Gaily, O gaily we glide and we sing,
We bear her along like a pearl on a string.

Softly, O softly we bear her along,
She hangs like a star in the dew of our song;
She springs like a beam on the brow of the tide,
She falls like a tear from the eyes of a bride.
Lightly, O lightly we glide and we sing,
We bear her along like a pearl on a string.

WANDERING SINGERS

(Written to one of their Tunes)

W<small>HERE</small> the voice of the wind calls our wandering feet,
Through echoing forest and echoing street,
With lutes in our hands ever-singing we roam,
All men are our kindred, the world is our home.

Our lays are of cities whose lustre is shed,
The laughter and beauty of women long dead;
The sword of old battles, the crown of old kings,
And happy and simple and sorrowful things.

What hope shall we gather, what dreams shall we sow?
Where the wind calls our wandering footsteps we go.
No love bids us tarry, no joy bids us wait:
The voice of the wind is the voice of our fate.

THE GOLDEN THRESHOLD

INDIAN WEAVERS

Weavers, weaving at break of day,
Why do you weave a garment so gay? ...
Blue as the wing of a halcyon wild,
We weave the robes of a new-born child.

Weavers, weaving at fall of night,
Why do you weave a garment so bright? ...
Like the plumes of a peacock, purple and green,
We weave the marriage-veils of a queen.

Weavers, weaving solemn and still,
What do you weave in the moonlight chill? ...
White as a feather and white as a cloud,
We weave a dead man's funeral shroud.

COROMANDEL FISHERS

Rise, brothers, rise, the wakening skies pray
    to the morning light,
The wind lies asleep in the arms of the dawn
    like a child that has cried all night.
Come, let us gather our nets from the shore,
    and set our catamarans free,
To capture the leaping wealth of the tide, for
    we are the sons of the sea.

No longer delay, let us hasten away in the
    track of the sea-gull's call,
The sea is our mother, the cloud is our brother,
    the waves are our comrades all.
What though we toss at the fall of the sun
    where the hand of the sea-god drives?
He who holds the storm by the hair, will hide
    in his breast our lives.

Sweet is the shade of the cocoanut glade, and
    the scent of the mango grove,
And sweet are the sands at the full o' the moon with the
    sound of the voices we love.
But sweeter, O brothers, the kiss of the spray
    and the dance of the wild foam's glee:
Row, brothers, row to the blue of the verge,
    where the low sky mates with the sea.

THE SNAKE-CHARMER

WHITHER dost thou hide from the magic of my flute-call?
In what moonlight-tangled meshes of perfume,
Where the clustering keovas guard the squirrel's slumber,
Where the deep woods glimmer with the jasmine's bloom?

I'll feed thee, O beloved, on milk and wild red honey,
I'll bear thee in a basket of rushes, green and white,
To a palace-bower where golden-vested maidens
Thread with mellow laughter the petals of delight.

Whither dost thou loiter, by what murmuring hollows,
Where oleanders scatter their ambrosial fire?
Come, thou subtle bride of my mellifluous wooing,
Come, thou silver-breasted moonbeam of desire!

CORN-GRINDERS

O little mouse, why dost thou cry
While merry stars laugh in the sky?

Alas! alas! my lord is dead!
Ah, who will ease my bitter pain?
He went to seek a millet-grain
In the rich farmer's granary shed;
They caught him in a baited snare,
And slew my lover unaware:
Alas! alas! my lord is dead.

O little deer, why dost thou moan,
Hid in thy forest-bower alone?

Alas! alas! my lord is dead!
Ah! who will quiet my lament?
At fall of eventide he went
To drink beside the river-head;
A waiting hunter threw his dart,
And struck my lover through the heart.
Alas! alas! my lord is dead.

O little bride, why dost thou weep
With all the happy world asleep?

Alas! alas! my lord is dead!
Ah, who will stay these hungry tears,
Or still the want of famished years,
And crown with love my marriage-bed?
My soul burns with the quenchless fire
That lit my lover's funeral pyre:
Alas! alas! my lord is dead.

THE GOLDEN THRESHOLD

VILLAGE-SONG

HONEY, child, honey, child, whither are you going?
Would you cast your jewels all to the breezes blowing?
Would you leave the mother who on golden grain has fed you?
Would you grieve the lover who is riding forth to wed you?

Mother mine, to the wild forest I am going,
Where upon the champa boughs the champa buds are blowing;
To the koil-haunted river-isles where lotus lilies glisten,
The voices of the fairy folk are calling me: O listen!

Honey, child, honey, child, the world is full of pleasure,
Of bridal-songs and cradle-songs and sandal-scented leisure.
Your bridal robes are in the loom, silver and saffron glowing,
Your bridal cakes are on the hearth: O whither are you going?

The bridal-songs and cradle-songs have cadences of sorrow,
The laughter of the sun to-day, the wind of death to-morrow.
Far sweeter sound the forest-notes where forest-streams are falling;
O mother mine, I cannot stay, the fairy-folk are calling.

IN PRAISE OF HENNA

A KOKILA called from a henna-spray:
Lira! Liree! Lira! Liree!
Hasten, maidens, hasten away
To gather the leaves of the henna-tree.
Send your pitchers afloat on the tide,
Gather the leaves ere the dawn be old,
Grind them in mortars of amber and gold,
The fresh green leaves of the henna-tree.

A kokila called from a henna-spray:
Lira! Liree! Lira! Liree!
Hasten maidens, hasten away
To gather the leaves of the henna-tree.
The tilka's red for the brow of a bride,
And betel-nut's red for lips that are sweet;
But, for lily-like fingers and feet,
The red, the red of the henna-tree.

HARVEST HYMN

Men's Voices

Lord of the lotus, lord of the harvest,
Bright and munificent lord of the morn!
Thine is the bounty that prospered our sowing,
Thine is the bounty that nurtured our corn.
We bring thee our songs and our garlands for tribute,
The gold of our fields and the gold of our fruit;
O giver of mellowing radiance, we hail thee,
We praise thee, O Surya, with cymbal and flute.

Lord of the rainbow, lord of the harvest,
Great and beneficent lord of the main!
Thine is the mercy that cherished our furrows,
Thine is the mercy that fostered our grain.
We bring thee our thanks and our garlands for tribute,
The wealth of our valleys, new-garnered and ripe;
O sender of rain and the dewfall, we hail thee,
We praise thee, Varuna, with cymbal and pipe.

Women's Voices

Queen of the gourd-flower, queen of the harvest,
Sweet and omnipotent mother, O Earth!
Thine is the plentiful bosom that feeds us,
Thine is the womb where our riches have birth.
We bring thee our love and our garlands for tribute,
With gifts of thy opulent giving we come;
O source of our manifold gladness, we hail thee,
We praise thee, O Prithvi, with cymbal and drum.

All Voices

Lord of the Universe, Lord of our being,
Father eternal, ineffable Om!
Thou art the Seed and the Scythe of our harvests,
Thou art our Hands and our Heart and our Home.
We bring thee our lives and our labours for tribute,
Grant us thy succour, thy counsel, thy care.
O Life of all life and all blessing, we hail thee,
We praise thee, O Bramha, with cymbal and prayer.

INDIAN LOVE-SONG

She

LIKE a serpent to the calling voice of flutes,
Glides my heart into thy fingers, O my Love!
Where the night-wind, like a lover, leans above
His jasmine-gardens and sirisha-bowers;
And on ripe boughs of many-coloured fruits
Bright parrots cluster like vermilion flowers.

He

Like the perfume in the petals of a rose,
Hides thy heart within my bosom, O my love!
Like a garland, like a jewel, like a dove
That hangs its nest in the asoka-tree.
Lie still, O love, until the morning sows
Her tents of gold on fields of ivory.

CRADLE-SONG

From groves of spice,
  O'er fields of rice,
Athwart the lotus-stream,
  I bring for you,
  Aglint with dew
A little lovely dream.

Sweet, shut your eyes,
  The wild fire-flies
Dance through the fairy neem;
  From the poppy-bole
  For you I stole
A little lovely dream.

Dear eyes, good-night,
  In golden light
The stars around you gleam;
  On you I press
  With soft caress
A little lovely dream.

SUTTEE

Lamp of my life, the lips of Death
Hath blown thee out with their sudden breath;
Naught shall revive thy vanished spark . . .
Love, must I dwell in the living dark?

Tree of my life, Death's cruel foot
Hath crushed thee down to thy hidden root;
Nought shall restore thy glory fled . . .
Shall the blossom live when the tree is dead?

Life of my life, Death's bitter sword
Hath severed us like a broken word,
Rent us in twain who are but one . .
Shall the flesh survive when the soul is gone?

SONGS FOR MUSIC

SONG OF A DREAM

Once in the dream of a night I stood
Lone in the light of a magical wood,
Soul-deep in visions that poppy-like sprang;
And spirits of Truth were the birds that sang,
And spirits of Love were the stars that glowed,
And spirits of Peace were the streams that flowed
In that magical wood in the land of sleep.

Lone in the light of that magical grove,
I felt the stars of the spirits of Love
Gather and gleam round my delicate youth,
And I heard the song of the spirits of Truth;
To quench my longing I bent me low
By the streams of the spirits of Peace that flow
In that magical wood in the land of sleep.

HUMAYUN TO ZOBEIDA

(From the Urdu)

You flaunt your beauty in the rose, your glory in the dawn,
Your sweetness in the nightingale, your whiteness in the swan.

You haunt my waking like a dream, my slumber like a moon,
Pervade me like a musky scent, possess me like a tune.

Yet, when I crave of you, my sweet, one tender moment's grace,
You cry, "*I sit behind the veil, I cannot show my face.*"

Shall any foolish veil divide my longing from my bliss?
Shall any fragile curtain hide your beauty from my kiss?

What war is this of *Thee* and *Me*? Give o'er the wanton strife,
You are the heart within my heart, the life within my life.

AUTUMN SONG

Like a joy on the heart of a sorrow,
  The sunset hangs on a cloud;
A golden storm of glittering sheaves,
Of fair and frail and fluttering leaves,
  The wild wind blows in a cloud.

Hark to a voice that is calling
  To my heart in the voice of the wind:
My heart is weary and sad and alone,
For its dreams like the fluttering leaves have gone,
  And why should I stay behind?

ALABASTER

Like this alabaster box whose art
Is frail as a cassia-flower, is my heart,
Carven with delicate dreams and wrought
With many a subtle and exquisite thought.

Therein I treasure the spice and scent
Of rich and passionate memories blent
Like odours of cinnamon, sandal and clove,
Of song and sorrow and life and love.

ECSTASY

Cover mine eyes, O my Love!
Mine eyes that are weary of bliss
As of light that is poignant and strong
O silence my lips with a kiss,
My lips that are weary of song!

Shelter my soul, O my love!
My soul is bent low with the pain
And the burden of love, like the grace
Of a flower that is smitten with rain:
O shelter my soul from thy face!

TO MY FAIRY FANCIES

Nay, no longer I may hold you,
   In my spirit's soft caresses,
Nor like lotus-leaves enfold you
   In the tangles of my tresses.
Fairy fancies, fly away
   To the white cloud-wildernesses,
     Fly away!

Nay, no longer ye may linger
   With your laughter-lighted faces,
Now I am a thought-worn singer
   In life's high and lonely places.
Fairy fancies, fly away,
   To bright wind-inwoven spaces,
     Fly away!

POEMS

ODE TO H.H. THE NIZAM OF HYDERABAD

(Presented at the Ramzan Durbar)

DEIGN, Prince, my tribute to receive,
This lyric offering to your name,
Who round your jewelled scepter bind
The lilies of a poet's fame;
Beneath whose sway concordant dwell
The peoples whom your laws embrace,
In brotherhood of diverse creeds,
And harmony of diverse race:

The votaries of the Prophet's faith,
Of whom you are the crown and chief
And they, who bear on Vedic brows
Their mystic symbols of belief;

And they, who worshipping the sun,
Fled o'er the old Iranian sea;
And they, who bow to Him who trod
The midnight waves of Galilee.

Sweet, sumptuous fables of Baghdad
The splendours of your court recall,
The torches of a Thousand Nights
Blaze through a single festival;
And Saki-singers down the streets,
Pour for us, in a stream divine,
From goblets of your love-ghazals
The rapture of your Sufi wine.

Prince, where your radiant cities smile,
Grim hills their sombre vigils keep,
Your ancient forests hoard and hold
The legends of their centuried sleep;
Your birds of peace white-pinioned float
O'er ruined fort and storied plain,
Your faithful stewards sleepless guard
The harvests of your gold and grain.

God give you joy, God give you grace
To shield the truth and smite the wrong,
To honour Virtue, Valour, Worth.
To cherish faith and foster song.
So may the lustre of your days
Outshine the deeds Firdusi sung,
Your name within a nation's prayer,
Your music on a nation's tongue.

LEILI

THE serpents are asleep among the poppies,
The fireflies light the soundless panther's way
To tangled paths where shy gazelles are straying,
And parrot-plumes outshine the dying day.
O soft! the lotus-buds upon the stream
Are stirring like sweet maidens when they dream.

A caste-mark on the azure brows of Heaven,
The golden moon burns sacred, solemn, bright
The winds are dancing in the forest-temple,
And swooning at the holy feet of Night.
Hush! in the silence mystic voices sing
And make the gods their incense-offering.

IN THE FOREST

Here, O my heart, let us burn the dear dreams that are dead,
Here in this wood let us fashion a funeral pyre
Of fallen white petals and leaves that are mellow and red,
Here let us burn them in noon's flaming torches of fire.

We are weary, my heart, we are weary, so long we have borne
The heavy loved burden of dreams that are dead, let us rest,
Let us scatter their ashes away, for a while let us mourn;
We will rest, O my heart, till the shadows are gray in the west.

But soon we must rise, O my heart, we must wander again
Into the war of the world and the strife of the throng;
Let us rise, O my heart, let us gather the dreams that remain,
We will conquer the sorrow of life with the sorrow of song.

PAST AND FUTURE

The new hath come and now the old retires:
And so the past becomes a mountain-cell,
Where lone, apart, old hermit-memories dwell
In consecrated calm, forgotten yet
Of the keen heart that hastens to forget
Old longings in fulfilling new desires.

And now the Soul stands in a vague, intense
Expectancy and anguish of suspense,
On the dim chamber-threshold . . . lo! he sees
Like a strange, fated bride as yet unknown,
His timid future shrinking there alone,
Beneath her marriage-veil of mysteries.

LIFE

Children, ye have not lived, to you it seems
Life is a lovely stalactite of dreams,
Or carnival of careless joys that leap
About your hearts like billows on the deep
In flames of amber and of amethyst.

Children, ye have not lived, ye but exist
Till some resistless hour shall rise and move
Your hearts to wake and hunger after love,
And thirst with passionate longing for the things
That burn your brows with blood-red sufferings.

Till ye have battled with great grief and fears,
And borne the conflict of dream-shattering years,
Wounded with fierce desire and worn with strife,
Children, ye have not lived: for this is life.

THE POET'S LOVE-SONG

In noon-tide hours, O Love, secure and strong,
   I need thee not; mad dreams are mine to bind
   The world to my desire, and hold the wind
A voiceless captive to my conquering song.
   I need thee not, I am content with these:
   Keep silence in thy soul, beyond the seas!

But in the desolate hour of midnight, when
   An ecstasy of starry silence sleeps
   On the still mountains and the soundless deeps,
And my soul hungers for thy voice, O then,
   Love, like the magic of wild melodies,
   Let thy soul answer mine across the seas.

TO THE GOD OF PAIN

Unwilling priestess in thy cruel fane,
Long hast thou held me, pitiless god of Pain,
Bound to thy worship by reluctant vows,
My tired breast girt with suffering, and my brows
Anointed with perpetual weariness.
Long have I borne thy service, through the stress
Of rigorous years, sad days and slumberless nights,
Performing thine inexorable rites.

For thy dark altars, balm nor milk nor rice,
But mine own soul thou'st ta'en for sacrifice:
All the rich honey of my youth's desire,
And all the sweet oils from my crushed life drawn,
And all my flower-like dreams and gem-like fire
Of hopes up-leaping like the light of dawn.

I have no more to give, all that was mine
Is laid, a wrested tribute, at thy shrine;
Let me depart, for my whole soul is wrung,
And all my cheerless orisons are sung;
Let me depart, with faint limbs let me creep
To some dim shade and sink me down to sleep.

THE SONG OF PRINCESS ZEB-UN-NISSA IN PRAISE OF HER OWN BEAUTY

(From the Persian)

WHEN from my cheek I lift my veil,
The roses turn with envy pale,
   And from their pierced hearts, rich with pain,
Send forth their fragrance like a wail.

Or if perchance one perfumed tress
Be lowered to the wind's caress,
   The honeyed hyacinths complain,
And languish in a sweet distress.

And, when I pause, still groves among,
(Such loveliness is mine) a throng
   Of nightingales awake and strain
Their souls into a quivering song.

INDIAN DANCERS

Eyes ravished with rapture, celestially panting, what passionate bosoms aflaming with fire
Drink deep of the hush of the hyacinth heavens that glimmer around them in fountains of light;
O wild and entrancing the strain of keen music that cleaveth the stars like a wail of desire,
And beautiful dancers with houri-like faces bewitch the voluptuous watches of night.

The scents of red roses and sandalwood flutter and die in the maze of their gem-tangled hair,
And smiles are entwining like magical serpents the poppies of lips that are opiate-sweet;
Their glittering garments of purple are burning like tremulous dawns in the quivering air,
And exquisite, subtle and slow are the tinkle and tread of their rhythmical, slumber-soft feet.

Now silent, now singing and swaying and swinging, like blossoms that bend to the breezes or showers,
Now wantonly winding, they flash, now they falter, and, lingering, languish in radiant choir;
Their jewel-girt arms and warm, wavering, lily-long fingers enchant through melodious hours,
Eyes ravished with rapture, celestially panting, what passionate bosoms aflaming with fire!

MY DEAD DREAM

Have you found me, at last, O my Dream?
   Seven aeons ago
You died and I buried you deep under forests of snow.
Why have you come hither? Who bade you
   awake from your sleep
And track me beyond the cerulean foam of the deep?

Would you tear from my lintels these sacred green
   garlands of leaves?
Would you scare the white, nested, wild pigeons
   of joy from my eaves?
Would you touch and defile with dead fingers the
   robes of my priest?
Would you weave your dim moan with the chantings
   of love at my feast?

Go back to your grave, O my Dream, under forests
   of snow,
Where a heart-riven child hid you once, seven
   aeons ago.
Who bade you arise from your darkness? I bid
   you depart!
Profane not the shrines I have raised in the
   clefts of my heart.

DAMAYANTE TO NALA IN THE HOUR OF EXILE

(A fragment)

SHALT thou be conquered of a human fate
My liege, my lover, whose imperial head
Hath never bent in sorrow of defeat?
Shalt thou be vanquished, whose imperial feet
Have shattered armies and stamped empires dead?
Who shall unking thee, husband of a queen?
Wear thou thy majesty inviolate.
Earth's glories flee of human eyes unseen,
Earth's kingdoms fade to a remembered dream,
But thine henceforth shall be a power supreme,
Dazzling command and rich dominion,
The winds thy heralds and thy vassals all
The silver-belted planets and the sun.
Where'er the radiance of thy coming fall,
Shall dawn for thee her saffron footcloths spread,
Sunset her purple canopies and red,
In serried splendour, and the night unfold
Her velvet darkness wrought with starry gold
For kingly raiment, soft as cygnet-down.
My hair shall braid thy temples like a crown
Of sapphires, and my kiss upon thy brows
Like cithar-music lull thee to repose,
Till the sun yield thee homage of his light.

O king, thy kingdom who from thee can wrest?
What fate shall dare uncrown thee from this breast,
O god-born lover, whom my love doth gird
And armour with impregnable delight
Of Hope's triumphant keen flame-carven sword?

THE QUEEN'S RIVAL

I

Queen Gulnaar sat on her ivory bed,
Around her countless treasures were spread;

Her chamber walls were richly inlaid
With agate, porphory, onyx and jade;

The tissues that veiled her delicate breast,
Glowed with the hues of a lapwing's crest;

But still she gazed in her mirror and sighed
"O King, my heart is unsatisfied."

King Feroz bent from his ebony seat:
"Is thy least desire unfulfilled, O Sweet?

"Let thy mouth speak and my life be spent
To clear the sky of thy discontent."

"I tire of my beauty, I tire of this
Empty splendour and shadowless bliss;

"With none to envy and none gainsay,
No savour or salt hath my dream or day."

Queen Gulnaar sighed like a murmuring rose:
"Give me a rival, O King Feroz."

II

King Feroz spoke to his Chief Vizier:
"Lo! ere to-morrow's dawn be here,

"Send forth my messengers over the sea,
To seek seven beautiful brides for me;

"Radiant of feature and regal of mien,
Seven handmaids meet for the Persian Queen."

* * * * *

Seven new moon tides at the Vesper call,
King Feroz led to Queen Gulnaar's hall

A young queen eyed like the morning star:
"I bring thee a rival, O Queen Gulnaar."

But still she gazed in her mirror and sighed:
"O King, my heart is unsatisfied."

Seven queens shone round her ivory bed,
Like seven soft gems on a silken thread,

Like seven fair lamps in a royal tower,
Like seven bright petals of Beauty's flower

Queen Gulnaar sighed like a murmuring rose
"Where is my rival, O King Feroz?"

III

When spring winds wakened the mountain floods,
And kindled the flame of the tulip buds,

When bees grew loud and the days grew long,
And the peach groves thrilled to the oriole's song,

Queen Gulnaar sat on her ivory bed,
Decking with jewels her exquisite head;

And still she gazed in her mirror and sighed:
"O King, my heart is unsatisfied."

Queen Gulnaar's daughter two spring times old,
In blue robes bordered with tassels of gold,

Ran to her knee like a wildwood fay,
And plucked from her hand the mirror away.

Quickly she set on her own light curls
Her mother's fillet with fringes of pearls;

Quickly she turned with a child's caprice
And pressed on the mirror a swift, glad kiss.

Queen Gulnaar laughed like a tremulous rose:
"Here is my rival, O King Feroz."

THE POET TO DEATH

Tarry a while, O Death, I cannot die
While yet my sweet life burgeons with its spring;
Fair is my youth, and rich the echoing boughs
Where *dhadikulas* sing.

Tarry a while, O Death, I cannot die
With all my blossoming hopes unharvested,
My joys ungarnered, all my songs unsung,
And all my tears unshed.

Tarry a while, till I am satisfied
Of love and grief, of earth and altering sky;
Till all my human hungers are fulfilled,
O Death, I cannot die!

THE INDIAN GIPSY

In tattered robes that hoard a glittering trace
Of bygone colours, broidered to the knee,
Behold her, daughter of a wandering race,
Tameless, with the bold falcon's agile grace,
And the lithe tiger's sinuous majesty.

With frugal skill her simple wants she tends,
She folds her tawny heifers and her sheep
On lonely meadows when the daylight ends,
Ere the quick night upon her flock descends
Like a black panther from the caves of sleep.

Time's river winds in foaming centuries
Its changing, swift, irrevocable course
To far off and incalculable seas;
She is twin-born with primal mysteries,
And drinks of life at Time's forgotten source.

TO MY CHILDREN

Jaya Surya, aetat 4

GOLDEN sun of victory, born
In my life's unclouded morn,
In my lambent sky of love,
May your growing glory prove
Sacred to your consecration,
To my heart and to my nation.
Sun of victory, may you be
Sun of song and liberty.

Padmaja, aetat 3

Lotus-maiden, you who claim
All the sweetness of your name,
Lakshmi, fortune's queen, defend you,
Lotus-born like you, and send you
Balmy moons of love to bless you,
Gentle joy-winds to caress you.
Lotus-maiden, may you be
Fragrant of all ecstasy.

Ranadheera, aetat 2

Little lord of battle, hail
In your newly-tempered mail!
Learn to conquer, learn to fight
In the foremost flanks of right,
Like Valmiki's heroes bold,
Rubies girt in epic gold.
Lord of battle, may you be,
Lord of love and chivalry.

Lilamani, aetat 1

Limpid jewel of delight
Severed from the tender night
Of your sheltering mother-mine,
Leap and sparkle, dance and shine,
Blithely and securely set
In love's magic coronet.
Living jewel, may you be
Laughter-bound and sorrow-free.

THE PARDAH NASHIN

Her life is a revolving dream
Of languid and sequestered ease;
Her girdles and her fillets gleam
Like changing fires on sunset seas;
Her raiment is like morning mist,
Shot opal, gold and amethyst.

From thieving light of eyes impure,
From coveting sun or wind's caress,
Her days are guarded and secure
Behind her carven lattices,
Like jewels in a turbaned crest,
Like secrets in a lover's breast.

But though no hand unsanctioned dares
Unveil the mysteries of her grace,
Time lifts the curtain unawares,
And Sorrow looks into her face . . .
Who shall prevent the subtle years,
Or shield a woman's eyes from tears?

TO YOUTH

O Youth, sweet comrade Youth, wouldst thou be gone?
Long have we dwelt together, thou and I;
Together drunk of many an alien dawn,
And plucked the fruit of many an alien sky.

Ah, fickle friend, must I, who yesterday
Dreamed forwards to long, undimmed ecstasy,
Henceforward dream, because thou wilt not stay,
Backward to transient pleasure and to thee?

I give thee back thy false, ephemeral vow;
But, O beloved comrade, ere we part,
Upon my mournful eyelids and my brow
Kiss me who hold thine image in my heart.

NIGHTFALL IN THE CITY OF HYDERABAD

See how the speckled sky burns like a pigeon's throat,
Jewelled with embers of opal and peridote.

See the white river that flashes and scintillates,
Curved like a tusk from the mouth of the city-gates.

Hark, from the minaret, how the muezzin's call
Floats like a battle-flag over the city wall.

From trellised balconies, languid and luminous
Faces gleam, veiled in a splendour voluminous.

Leisurely elephants wind through the winding lanes,
Swinging their silver bells hung from their silver chains.

Round the high Char Minar sounds of gay cavalcades
Blend with the music of cymbals and serenades.

Over the city bridge Night comes majestical,
Borne like a queen to a sumptuous festival.

STREET CRIES

When dawn's first cymbals beat upon the sky,
Rousing the world to labour's various cry,
To tend the flock, to bind the mellowing grain,
From ardent toil to forge a little gain,
And fasting men go forth on hurrying feet,
buy bread, buy bread, rings down the eager street.

When the earth falters and the waters swoon
With the implacable radiance of noon,
And in dim shelters koils hush their notes,
And the faint, thirsting blood in languid throats
Craves liquid succour from the cruel heat,
buy fruit, buy fruit, steals down the panting street.

When twilight twinkling o'er the gay bazaars,
Unfurls a sudden canopy of stars,
When lutes are strung and fragrant torches lit
On white roof-terraces where lovers sit
Drinking together of life's poignant sweet,
Buy Flowers, Buy Flowers, floats down the singing street.

TO INDIA

O YOUNG through all thy immemorial years!
Rise, Mother, rise, regenerate from thy gloom,
And, like a bride high-mated with the spheres,
Beget new glories from thine ageless womb!

The nations that in fettered darkness weep
Crave thee to lead them where great mornings break...
Mother, O Mother, wherefore dost thou sleep?
Arise and answer for thy children's sake!

Thy Future calls thee with a manifold sound
To crescent honours, splendours, victories vast;
Waken, O slumbering Mother and be crowned,
Who once wert empress of the sovereign Past.

THE ROYAL TOMBS OF GOLCONDA

I MUSE among these silent fanes
Whose spacious darkness guards your dust;
Around me sleep the hoary plains
That hold your ancient wars in trust.
I pause, my dreaming spirit hears,
Across the wind's unquiet tides,
The glimmering music of your spears,
The laughter of your royal brides.

In vain, O Kings, doth time aspire
To make your names oblivion's sport,
While yonder hill wears like a tier
The ruined grandeur of your fort.
Though centuries falter and decline,
Your proven strongholds shall remain
Embodied memories of your line,
Incarnate legends of your reign.

O Queens, in vain old Fate decreed
Your flower-like bodies to the tomb;
Death is in truth the vital seed
Of your imperishable bloom
Each new-born year the bulbuls sing
Their songs of your renascent loves;
Your beauty wakens with the spring
To kindle these pomegranate groves.

TO A BUDDHA SEATED ON A LOTUS

Lord Buddha, on thy Lotus-throne,
With praying eyes and hands elate,
What mystic rapture dost thou own,
Immutable and ultimate?
What peace, unravished of our ken,
Annihilate from the world of men?

The wind of change for ever blows
Across the tumult of our way,
To-morrow's unborn griefs depose
The sorrows of our yesterday.
Dream yields to dream, strife follows strife,
And Death unweaves the webs of Life.

For us the travail and the heat,
The broken secrets of our pride,
The strenuous lessons of defeat,
The flower deferred, the fruit denied;
But not the peace, supremely won,
Lord Buddha, of thy Lotus-throne.

With futile hands we seek to gain
Our inaccessible desire,
Diviner summits to attain,
With faith that sinks and feet that tire;
But nought shall conquer or control
The heavenward hunger of our soul.

The end, elusive and afar,
Still lures us with its beckoning flight,
And all our mortal moments are
A session of the Infinite.
How shall we reach the great, unknown
Nirvana of thy Lotus-throne?

Printed in Great Britain
by Amazon